Note to parents, carers and teachers

Read it yourself is a series of modern stories, favourite characters and traditional tales written in a simple way for children who are learning to read. The books can be read independently or as part of a guided reading session.

Each book is carefully structured to include many high-frequency words vital for first reading. The sentences on each page are supported closely by pictures to help with understanding, and to offer lively details to talk about.

The books are graded into four levels that progressively introduce wider vocabulary and longer stories as a reader's ability and confidence grows.

Ideas for use

- Although your child will now be progressing towards silent, independent reading, let her know that your help and encouragement is always available.

- Developing readers can be concentrating so hard on the words that they sometimes don't fully grasp the meaning of what they're reading. Answering the puzzle questions at the back of the book will help with understanding.

For more information and advice on Read it yourself and book banding, visit **www.ladybird.com/readityourself**

Book
Band
10

Level 4 is ideal for children who are ready to read longer stories with a wider vocabulary and are eager to start reading independently.

Special features:

Detailed illustrations to capture the imagination

Clear type

Longer sentences

Full, exciting story

Sweet Tooth and the Glumps took Oddie to Main Street. The same Moshlings called to Oddie, but Oddie did not look at them. He just looked at the Hypno Blaster

"Something is wrong with Oddie!" the Moshlings said.

30

31

Suddenly Sweet Tooth said, "I want some candy – now!"

While the Glumps looked for some candy, Hansel got Oddie with his candy cane.

"What...?" said Oddie. He was out of the trance!

36

37

Educational Consultant: Geraldine Taylor
Book Banding Consultant: Kate Ruttle

A catalogue record for this book is available from the British Library

This edition published by Ladybird Books Ltd 2014
80 Strand, London, WC2R 0RL
A Penguin Company

001

ISBN: 978-0-72328-093-4

Printed in China

Oddie
The Hero

Written by Ronne Randall

Illustrated by Vincent Bechet

"It's going to be a good day!"
said Oddie. He was going
to talk to Roary Scrawl and
Roary was going to write
about Oddie in his newspaper.

Oddie looked at Roary Scrawl's letter.
The letter called Oddie a hero
– he had saved some Sparklepops
from two Glumps. Oddie could be
on the front page of the newspaper!

Oddie had saved the Sparklepops from two Glumps, called Podge and Fabio. The Glumps were picking on the Moshlings. Oddie had to help them!

Oddie had blasted Podge and Fabio with sweets and both Glumps had run away.

The Sparklepops had cheered, "You're a hero, Oddie!"

On the way to the newspaper office, a candy cane suddenly grabbed Oddie.

"What...?" he said.

It was Oddie's friend Hansel. "Look out!" said Hansel. "There could be Glumps about!"

But Oddie wanted to get to the newspaper office, so he left Hansel there.

On Main Street, some Moshlings came up to Oddie. "You're a hero!" the Moshlings said.

Oddie talked with them and took some pictures, too.

When Oddie got to the newspaper office, Roary Scrawl was not there.

"What's going on?" Oddie said.

Suddenly Sweet Tooth, Podge and Fabio came in!

Oddie was trapped! He was scared and called out for Roary.

"Roary is not here," said Sweet Tooth, "and he didn't write you a letter, we did – so we could trap you here. Now we can get back at you for scaring the Glumps away from the Sparklepops."

Sweet Tooth told Oddie to take them to his home.
"We can get your friends, too!" said Sweet Tooth.
"No! Not my friends!" said Oddie.

UNDER CONSTRUCTION

27

Oddie didn't want to take Sweet Tooth and the Glumps to his home. So Sweet Tooth put Oddie in a trance with a Hypno Blaster.

"I've got you now!" said Sweet Tooth.

Sweet Tooth and the Glumps took Oddie to Main Street. The same Moshlings called to Oddie, but Oddie did not look at them. He just looked at the Hypno Blaster.

"Something is wrong with Oddie!" the Moshlings said.

31

On the way to Oddie's home,
Sweet Tooth saw Hansel.

"Take him, too!" Sweet Tooth said.
"We want all the sweets we can get!"

Podge and Fabio grabbed Hansel.

Hansel talked to Oddie when the Glumps were not looking. But Oddie did not look at Hansel or talk to him.

Suddenly Sweet Tooth said,
"I want some candy – now!"

While Podge and Fabio looked
for some candy, Hansel got
Oddie with his candy cane.

"What...?" said Oddie.
He was out of the trance!

Oddie now saw what was going
on and came up with a plan.
When the Glumps were not looking,
he told his plan to Hansel.

While Hansel left a trail of sweet crumbs, Oddie took Sweet Tooth and the Glumps to some trees. When they came away from the trees, they were suddenly at...

...the Volcano!

While Oddie and Hansel cheered, Elder Furi and his helpers rounded up Sweet Tooth and the Glumps.

Roary Scrawl was there, too. He took a picture of Oddie and Hansel.

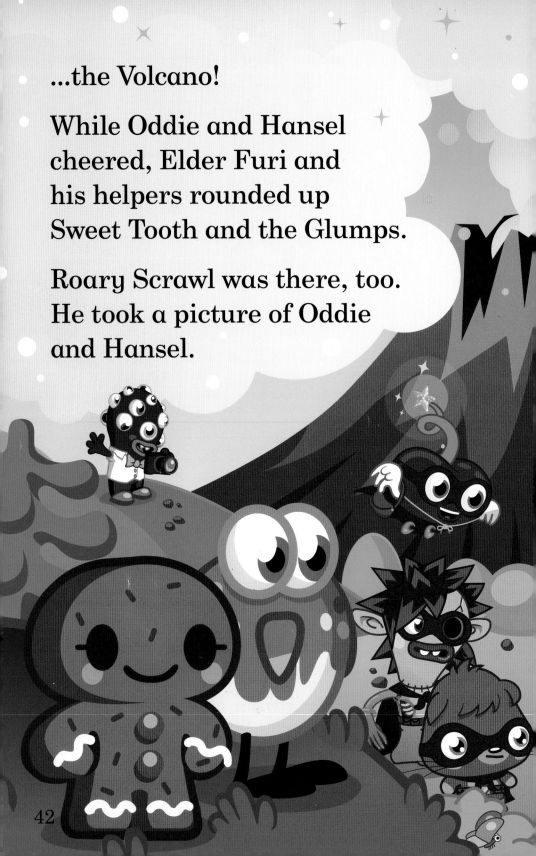

"Some Moshlings told me something was wrong," said Roary, "so I followed the crumb trail. I'm going to put you both on the front page of my newspaper!"

Now Oddie really was a hero – and so was Hansel!

How much do you remember about the story of Moshi Monsters: Oddie the Hero? Answer these questions and find out!

- Who is Oddie going to see at the beginning of the story?

- Why is he going to be in the newspaper?

- Who does Oddie see on the way to the newspaper office?

- Who has tricked Oddie?

- How does Hansel get Oddie out of the trance?

- Where do Oddie and Hansel end up taking Sweet Tooth and the Glumps?

Unjumble these words to make characters from the story, then match them to the correct pictures.

Oedid   Helsan   Stewe Thoot

Rayor Slawrc   Pegdo   Foabi

Read it yourself with Ladybird

Tick the books you've read!

For more confident readers who can read simple stories with help.

Level 3

☐ ☐ ☐ ☐ ☐ ☐

☐ ☐ ☐ ☐ ☐ ☐ ☐ ☐

Longer stories for more independent, fluent readers.

Level 4

☐ ☐ ☐ ☐ ☐ ☐

☐ ☐ ☐ ☐ ☐ ☐ ☐ ☐